Perfection, perfection
What is perfection?

Can it be achieved?

By James R. Heriford

Cover by Carol Berhorst
Sketches by Rose Hoyle
Photos by J. R. Heriford

ISBN 978-0-6152-3687-2
Copy write 2008
By James R. Heriford

I would like to dedicate this book to all the pastors and evangelists that are anxious to arrive in heaven and meet all the people they have led to join the church. And all those who are waiting to be seated beside the throne of God as though they have deserved a front seat. Especially to those that mastered a great vocabulary of ministerial words and they arrive before God and He will ask for explanations of those marvelous words that were developed by humans to look good and pharisaical.

I hope and pray these people do not find they walked in the wrong gate but just find the ones they expected to see were busy waiting on The Lord and had no concern for them. Ego is a great destroyer of a good life and it is evidence of worldly thinking.

What do you as pastor expect of the members of your church? Are they to be perfect in your eyes or the eyes of the Lord?

Contents

Introduction	5
Perfect day	6
Life	7
Night	11
Vacation	12
Marriage	13
Child	14
Job	15
Church	16
Automobile	18
Righteousness	20
Be attitudes	27
Perfection achievement	37
What does the Bible teach	41
Heaven	71
My testimony	75

Perfection?

I have never been a perfectionist but I have known some. Having been in Africa and witnessed the 'perfection' of the joyful people there I had to rethink the 'idea' of perfection. What is it and who determines its value? I have come to the conclusion that it is controlled by time and trends. Imagination may play a big part in it. Yesterdays' idea went by the wayside when today arrived. Is life and faith that flexible? Or do we just take advantage of someone else's thinking because it looks better or sounds better? Is it like listening to the sales pitch and then making the decision? Loyalty to what ever comes into the picture may sound like the easy road but is it?

As you read this think seriously about the 'perfection' in your life and the things that really mater.

Webster's New World Dictionary says: 1. the act or process of perfecting, 2. the quality or condition of being perfect; extreme degree of excellence according to a given standard, 3. a person or thing that is the perfect embodiment of some quality.

A perfect day?

Since I am retired and often have free time I enjoy setting on my front porch and listening to the birds and watching the traffic go by. On a nice clear day with a temperature that is reasonable I can easily think of it as a perfect day to enjoy Gods world. When the temperature is below freezing it is not so easy to feel like it is that perfect day but what is the perfect day? Maybe with a little snow to make things look clean or a sunny day to feel the warmth of the sun but every day will be perfect for someone somewhere. I like to fish and a perfect day for me is one with very little wind to disturb the water. A few clouds to keep the sun from getting too hot on my brow or back would be OK but too many clouds seem to ruin a good day for fishing. I like to work on things such as cars or lawn mowers but a sun that glares can be a hazard for seeing the work. What would a perfect day be for you?

I hope no one minds but I can't help but mention our days in the little country of Malawi. It was dry even during the rainy season. Two or three inches of rain would soak into the ground fast and the air would be dry again. I never felt a cold day because the temperature was seldom below fifty degrees and it never got above a temperature that we could not endure as long as we were out of the sun. True it was not always perfect and as I read the news I am reminded of the flooding that took place in the low areas of the country. For me each day was perfect and I dream of being there again.

I was reminded of the 30s and 40s when we had little or nothing and were not suffering by having to turn the crank to open or close the car windows. Turning the crank to start the car was not a chore but the natural thing to do. Was that too much for us humans? Is work that degrading? As I hear people complain of the high cost of gasoline I wonder what those in the 20s thought about travel to a neighbors' house that was five miles away. A days' journey was common for them and we complain about the cost of gas or an airplane ticket. When will we reach perfection?

A perfect life?

In the 83 years I have been on this earth I cannot remember a day that I would consider my life as worthless or without some interesting events. I enjoyed school and excelled in most classes and enjoyed printing class at Wyandotte High School. My time in the service was a great learning experience and I enjoyed learning to fly. As Georgia and I witnessed the life of people in

Africa we felt like they were being left out of a joyful life but to them every day was a day of action and excitement.

A search for food for the day; hope for a job to earn a little money for food; a place to rest on the 5 mile journey to work. I believe they were the happiest people I ever met. Was that a perfect life?

I think greed has become a great stumbling block for many people that are searching for that perfect life. The need for a nicer home, a better car or maybe a nice boat, to spend the weekend on the lake, with others that have those things and that can be a false hope.

As a youth I spent several weeks on an uncles' farm and experienced a life that to me was near perfect. When it was harvest time all the farmers and neighbors got together to gather in the harvest. It was not by request or invitation it was just a way of life and caring for each other. If a farmer had an illness others came to help with the chores. This was true of the ladies, as well as the men since feeding all of them during harvest became a major project. It was a matter of helping each other survive and making the most of the harvest.

How much better is life with all the things we wish for?

'Christmas season' brings a lot of questions to my thinking. As I hear people talking about shopping for toys or things I wonder what the purpose of it all is. Do we just need to spend money or do we really understand what the meaning of Christmas is and what it is all about? The real purpose of the Christmas season is to remember the Christ Child that became our Savior and the real reason for the Season. It seems to me that we have forgotten the real gift from above. I have thought often of trying to start a campaign to eliminate the celebration of Christmas as it now is or at least to change the way we celebrate.

I was raised in a Christian home. My father was a Baptist minister and my mother was a devoted wife and mother that raised and taught seven children and read and taught us the Bible. We were not exposed to worldly things as some might have been but we were told of the trouble they could bring.

I began to see the effects of drinking alcohol when I entered the service in 1943 and witnessed the effect it had on service men that had learned to drink at home and were addicted to it by the time they joined the army. As I looked at some who were so inebriated that they could not walk I was shocked that others thought it was funny to see them stumble about. Many nights were spent dragging them to their bunks and tucking them in. I felt sorrow for them and wanted to take pictures of them so they could see how foolish they were. I cannot see how anyone would consider that a good life. Several I knew were dropped from the cadet program because of the drinking problem.

At the same time I witnessed the effects of promiscuity as some that were married were looking for 'fun' in town while their wives were at home trying to stay alive on what they could earn at home. <u>For some fun was not what they received.</u>

I remember an oft quoted line of a friend whose wife watched soap operas a lot; "life can be beautiful 'with Johns other wife". It seems faithfulness is not important to some and I think a lot of the worlds' trouble with juveniles is the result of such action. I have friends that wonder why their child or children have gone astray while they try to pacify them with toys, anything they ask for or maybe some they didn't want but parents thought it would get them in good with the child. It is impossible to buy 'perfection' or happiness but a lot of love can bring it to reality very well.

A perfect night?

I spent last night, October 21, setting on my porch watching the clouds disappear in the darkness. It was 70 degrees with a very light breeze and the traffic was very light so the silence of the night was not interrupted with the noise of the cars going by. It was cloudy enough that I saw very few stars but the moon glittered through at times to brighten the evening. As I enjoyed that quiet time I thought of how God must be pleased with His creation of this perfect night and I was enjoying it with Him.

I have never had an interest in partying as some seem to think is necessary to enjoy life. I often listen to the scanner in the evening and have been amazed at the number of calls the police have for domestic disturbances. It might be husband and wife or even a youth in the family that has become unruly but in either case the situation is disturbing to me. In most cases the problem develops from alcohol. On one occasion a father was called to inform him his son had been picked up drunk and uncontrollable and they needed his help. His response was "throw him in jail and lock the door". It is sad when family members mean so little to parents and the parents may be the real problem in the first place.

A perfect vacation?

If you have ever spent a week or even a month on a vacation away from home you know the joy of returning home to your own bed. There is something about home that we cherish and are glad to return to or at lest we should be. A vacation is a time when we can get away from the trials and worry of every day life and work; a time to relax and restore our strength for another year. But for many of us the restoration is not what we accomplish. We get home exhausted and wish the week had been longer. I have learned that the perfect vacation is one with a purpose but not for selfish outcome. Having spent time in New Mexico working with the Navaho we realized a time of relaxing and at the same time accomplishing something worthwhile and it was very relaxing and did not leave us exhausted.

A trip to Pelstan, Michigan to help repair a church building and hold Bible School for the children was a joyful experience and a time to meet new friends. Our stay in Malawi was very enjoyable and we were saddened at having to leave new friends but returning home was exciting as well coming home relaxed and ready to go back to work. What determines a true and perfect vacation for you?

A perfect marriage?

I have heard many people say they had a perfect marriage. But what was perfect about it? I would consider the 59.5 years Georgia and I spent together as a perfect marriage but how perfect was it? We raised five children and enjoyed all of them as they grew to adulthood and began to raise their own little ones. I was never without a job. But not every thing was perfect. The need for a home meant money had to be accumulated for materials and that was not easy when clothing was needed for kids as well as every day necessities.

When material was available the hours of work to build a house took time away from home life and giving attention to wife and children. Tension arose many times over where was the money going and was it necessary. Then came the times I was tired and wanted to get away from sixteen hour days and do a little fishing. Why was I not working on the house? Georgia had some difficult times trying to understand life but was very gracious and we survived for many years even with the little things that we could not agree on. A perfect marriage? Yes I think so because we enjoyed many things together even in our old age and were able to take part in several Mission trips together that brought great joy to all of us and still do as those images run through my mind again.

A perfect child?

Oh yes, our children were perfect. Just ask grandma. I learned years ago that to get in to get acquainted with new people you first ask about their grandchildren and they immediately grab the photos. Yes everyone has perfect children but they can go astray. I once heard it said that if you look at a man's life you can see what his son will be like. At the same time I know that some have a totally different view of what a good child is like. It may be a son that excels in football or a daughter that excels in learning and trying to become a doctor. We all expect our children to excel but often on our own personal desires and not what they would prefer in life.

Many parents have high hopes for their children and 'push' them to excel. It becomes their dream and not that of the child. I realize some children need a little coaxing to reach their potential but 'pushing' them to accomplish the <u>parents</u> goal can often be devastating for the child and not accomplish their real potential. Love is essential for every family and love can make a great difference in the outcome of a child's accomplishments.

A perfect Job?

I at one time had a coffee cup that had a message inscribed on it that said "Doing what you love is success" the other side said "Loving what you do is success". As I left the army air corpse I was excited about commercial flying and hoped to get into it in some way but instead I went to a print shop and never left printing until I was too old to do anything else. I did do some flying on a fun basis and for the Civil Air Patrol but not commercially. For 50 some years I fully enjoyed being in the printing business and even have the opportunity to practice it as mission work overseas as a printer. To me that was the perfect job and a real joy. Even though my first employer was an atheist and very rude and vulgar I enjoyed the work and I felt I may have had some impact on his attitude in life. I hope what you are doing is as rewarding. If not I hope you will find the place where you can enjoy your work and make it a part of your ministry for Christ.

The perfect church?

As I look back over the years The Lord has allowed me to be active I have seen many churches and realized they were all different. My idea of a perfect church is one that does just what Jesus taught us all to do and that was to minister to people just as He was doing when He was here on earth. I am convinced that many churches are failing in that task and wish I could do something to encourage them to take a real heartfelt concern for the people in their community. As Jesus talked to a scholar that had asked "what is the greatest commandment", Jesus replied that the greatest is to love the Lord your God with all your heart and your neighbor as yourself. That is what Jesus did and told us to do. A glass of water, an ear to listen or a helping hand can do wonders if it is a step in love. Remember what 'Webster' said; "the act or process of perfecting". We cannot always be perfect but we can strive to that goal. It may begin with a little smile that says I like you as you are. That smile might be the first step to a new relationship.

I know of churches that have failed completely in their appointed task by being concerned about the number of names on the church role instead of ministering to those that God had placed in their parish for them. It seems the important thing is to enlarge the church or spend the money on decorating rather than building a ministry that will help people in the neighborhood. One church that had meant so much to me early in life recently closed its doors for that reason. How sad.

The perfect retirement?

I never cease to be amazed at the fact that we think of retirement as a time to set and do nothing. Or maybe to catch up on the fishing we seldom had time for. WOW what a dream. It seems the more we try to relax the more things need fixing. The longer we stay in bed the harder it is to get up and do what needs to be done.

It is nice to have the opportunity to travel and visit sights we always wanted to see. Hawaiian Islands, the ocean or even travel overseas but the real value of those journeys lies in what it accomplishes and who benefits from them. Some have even attempted to totally relax and do nothing at retirement only to die from "not doing". Others have found great joy in volunteer work that can minister to people in some way. Many volunteer in hospitals, nursing homes and as helpers to people that have difficulty getting around. Not only are they being useful they are finding life has greater meaning for them. Retirement is a great time to get involved in missions and there is always a need for people to minister both local and overseas. Remember God said He would supply the needs if we are willing to go.

The perfect automobile?

I will never cease to be amazed at the variety of cars on the street. Every morning as eight AM approaches I see at least five hundred cars go by my house. I live on a busy street and sit on my porch many mornings to watch the traffic and the birds. The cars delivering people to work and the birds hoping to spot a worm or a bite to eat make a very interesting way to pass the morning. There is such a variety of shapes and sizes of cars that I wonder who can design so many different vehicles.

I remember years ago when cars were all very 'square' and each year some manufacturer designed some thing more attractive to sell better. Soon the cars became like rockets that would race through the air with very little resistance. That was a big selling point but to me it was a waste of space, as the cars became very narrow at the top, so two people were in a crowded position for riding. As the years went by it became a race to build something that was more attractive to the buyer without considering the practicality of it. Now the new Chrysler cars are back to 'blunt fronts and backs and I suggest that they are just as efficient as the more streamlined cars.

I at one time drove a BMW Iseta that was a very small car with a single cylinder engine and one seat just wide enough for two people. The front of the car was the only door and it caused many eyes to take a second look.

It was the perfect car at the time as I was driving several miles to work and it would go 50 miles on a gallon of gas. I wish I had it now with the new price of gasoline. A perfect automobile is as 'relevant' as life itself. If it fits wear it, if it fits your need it is the perfect car. As long as you can afford it, it is your choice. My choice of cars has varied from time to time and usually because of family needs. If you think you have the perfect car more power to you. Like many things in life our concerns change as life changes but one thing should never change and that is our choice to be what Christ designed us to be. Do you shop around to find the right religion or the finest church? Forget that and just listen for the Masters instruction and He will give you just the thing to bring joy to life. I led a Bible Study at Lincoln University Baptist Student Union several years ago when a young man was the director. He had no car and asked the students to pray for a car for him so he could get around town to take care of business. The next day an old car appeared ion the parking lot and he called the police to get it removed and as they checked for the owner it turned out to be registered in his name. He wasn't expecting God to answer that way but drove that old car for several weeks till he could get something a little newer. God does answer prayers though not as we expect sometimes.

The perfect righteousness?

Righteousness, goodness, sinless life but what is true righteousness? Is yours different from mine? Does everyone make their own laws as far as righteousness is concerned? It seems that each generation develops a different opinion of how we should conduct ourselves. What is sin and what is not? What can I do and get by with it? I fear we have become so self sufficient and complacent that our only concern is self and maybe family. Neighbors no longer are a part of our concerns.

I have known many preachers including my own father and found as much variety in them as the marbles in a boys' bag. As I listen to them I try to learn as much as possible but at the same time I want to tell them to make things a little clearer so I can understand their point. One pastor very often said we have to be 'doing Gods' work' and I agreed but he never said what Gods' work was. Another would say to be a Christian we had to 'do the will of God' but never could tell me what the will of God was.

If pastors would spend more time helping the members find their place in Gods' plan it would be much easier for them to understand 'the will of God'. We all have different abilities and interests and the fervent pastor can be a big help in guiding those abilities. One person may be able to provide transportation to the doctor or the store. Another may be a good seamstress that could make things for those in need. Telephones are always a great way to minister and most anyone can do that. <u>Don't tell them to 'do the works of God' show</u>

them how. The story of the giving a fish to help someone is very true but if we fail to tell him how to fish we have 'missed the boat'.

Several years ago we used a book study to help people find their place in Gods' service. It was based on a story of a garbage collector that found his place in the riches of Christ by just being a kind and courteous garbage collector. He did not preach but he showed the works of Christ by his life at work. In the study we were all asked to list the things we liked to do or were able to do and then put them to the test in some ministry that set an example of Christian ministry. God has a way of making use of any effort we put forth if it is in an attitude of love. Let Him use you and you will be fully blest.

Is righteousness as simple as that? I have been visited by a group of a different denomination than mine but they talk of preparing for the coming of the Kingdom. They teach 'Christ as the Son of God and the savior of man' but are they really righteous? Can we all have different views of God and still be righteous? Can we differ in our understanding of the Book of Revelation and still be righteous?

There are many interpretations of what constitutes righteousness and I fear some are very dangerous. Some people say we are all going to the same place. Some think it makes no difference what denomination we are a part of we are all worshiping the same God. I fear we all have the wrong idea of what Christ taught when He was on this earth. I don't find anywhere in the Bible that Jesus taught the disciples how to build a church building but He taught them how to minister to people. Every where Jesus went He physically ministered to someone in some way. He healed the sick, He raised the dead and He raised the spirits of people that were hurting in a multitude of ways.

Maybe I have been a Baptist too long but I have a feeling that too many Baptists as well as others have forgotten the meaning of what Jesus taught.

Why have a large congregation if it is not accomplishing the task God assigned to them. As I watch television and see the very large churches with multitudes gathered for worship I begin to wonder if they are doing what God has for them to do or are they there to see a great performance? Jesus went about doing 'good' and I am convinced that is what He taught His followers to do. The more I see those crowds the more I wonder if the purpose of it all is to raise money for the speaker or the church and very little goes to ministry. As a preacher on television takes time to ask for donations I instantly wonder if he trusts God for those things. Maybe it is time they begin to rely on God and the need for begging will no longer stand in the way of their ministry.

I wonder often if anyone is ever very near to perfection. Jesus realized that humans had a difficult time being 'good' or righteous. He also new it was because we were human and God had given us the choice of obedience or disobedience. I don't know why He did it but He did and now we have to live with it. He did not leave us there though as He sent His only son to show what love could do. As Jesus ministered to people He painted a picture of <u>what we could be like if we wished</u>. It was made plain that we could rejoice with Him if we would just be like Him and a joy it would be.

As I have been studying the beatitudes I think of several things Jesus said in His ministry on this earth. As He spoke of praying He said our praying should be done in secret. Not because we didn't want others to know what we pray about but because it is something that comes from the heart. You might not want the president listening in on you phone but God listens to all our conversation and prayer. What are the beatitudes but an approach to changing attitudes? Be-attitudes. Jesus wants us to realize that our actions and words were the things that, coming from the heart, made the difference in our lives and not always what people could see on the outside. Micah 6:8 says "what does the Lord require of you but to do justly, to love mercy and to walk humbly with your God"

To start let us look at the word be- attitudes. I know it is not separated that way in the Bible but I think we should look at it in that way. You see Christ had a difficult time convincing His followers there was a difference in looking good and being good. Even the leaders in the temple and synagogue looked good and were convinced that was all that was necessary. Jesus had a better way.

I remember a story I once heard of a farmer selling a horse to a fellow but when the fellow tried to get the horse to go it wouldn't move. The farmer said wait a minute and picked up a 2x4 and hit the horse across the head and it soon began to go. The fellow said why did you do that? And the farmer said you just have to change his attitude. Jesus had to do that with some who heard Him but He did it with Love. In other words if our attitudes are right the next step is easy.

In another situation Jesus pointed to those that were too anxious to get things going and did not wait for the Holy Spirit and His instructions. King Saul had a problem with that and went ahead with his plans only to be rebuked by the prophet Samuel. God punished Saul for that action very seriously.

Again I am reminded of the preacher that had to sell his horse. He had trained the horse to respond to 'Christian words'. An excited neighbor, thinking that the horse must be good because of its training, came to buy the horse and the preacher told him that to get the horse to go you just say 'Praise the Lord'. That was easy but to stop the horse you say 'Halelulya'. So the man got on the horse and it took off in a trot as soon as he said 'Praise the Lord'. That was great until he saw they were headed for a deep ravine and he yelled 'halelulya' and the horse stopped right on the edge of the bluff. Being very frightened he wiped his forehead and said 'Praise the Lord'. Some times we don't wait to get full instructions.

Remember also that attitudes can change and we need to be always alert to our attitudes that they remain true to Christ's teachings. It was a problem for Paul as he tried to guide the early church. Some would be led astray by a false teacher that was welcomed by those that had itching ears. Any improvement sounded good but was not. We seem to want and expect improvements to everything in life but that can be dangerous.

That reminds me of the story of the new and improved jetliner that was making its first flight. The plane was loaded and had taxied to the runway to take off when the computer on board made the announcement that the plane was totally controlled by the computer and would take off, climb to its required altitude, and immediately head for its destination. After take off the computer again began to announce the agenda and stated there was nothing to worry about for nothing could go wrong, go wrong, go wrong! New technology may be great but a 'new righteousness' is not.

The Beatitudes

<u>Blessed are the 'poor in spirit' for theirs is the kingdom of Heaven</u>.

Jesus did not mean those that were not 'spiritual' but rather those that were humble. Why did He say "theirs is the kingdom of Heaven"? I visit with some of the Jehovah Witnesses often and as you know they believe that the Kingdom of God is still to come. I believe the Kingdom of God came as I put my trust in Him and His Spirit now dwells in me. The Kingdom of God is within us when we believe that He is and He is the Son of God and let Him be our guide from that time on. Be our guide? Yes, our guide in all we do whether at home, work or where ever we venture, if we are continually listening for His voice. Fifteen minutes a day in prayer? No, <u>continually</u> in contact with the wisdom only God can give. Fifteen minutes of righteousness is not enough and with out His help we cannot be righteous the rest of the day.

Yes ours is the Kingdom of Heaven because we let God be our guide and not try to be righteous on our own. His Holy Spirit will tell us in some subtle way when someone needs our concern and when he does we need to respond.

The beatitudes are attitudes that we develop as we grow closer to the Lord and once we have achieved them we cannot go back. When Georgia and I were in Malawi several years ago she had an experience that she, nor I, will ever forget. While visiting a village to plan a women's meeting, an elderly lady was climbing down from the corn bin where they stored their years' supply of corn. A home made ladder leaned against the bamboo bin and the cover was off so the lady could fill a bushel basket with ears of corn.

After the basket was full she put it on top of her head and climbed down and carried the basket on her head to the yard where children were waiting to shuck the ears. Realizing Georgia's amazement the lady emptied the basket and carried it to Georgia and set it on her head. As expected it fell off very soon. This woman had practiced doing that since she was a child and it had become second nature to her. I think if we practiced being 'poor', 'merciful' and all the beatitudes it would no longer be an occasional thing but so natural that it would actually be our life. Not just on occasion but continually.

Paul in writing to the Ephesians said "I strive toward the mark". He knew he was not perfect but he was working to that end with God's help and only God could make the difference.

Perfection cannot be achieved instantly or over night but has to be strived for. We cannot expect our children to be perfect at birth but we help them grow toward that end. As new people enter our fellowship we are to help them grow, not to be just like us but as God would like them to be. As I look at my neighbor I can easily say he is not perfect but neither can I make him perfect. I can try to help him grow to that end if I can learn to love him and understand his life and realize God made him different from me for a reason. I have experienced times when my life seemed to affect the lives of others. As I mention earlier, a man I worked for was very vulgar and rude even when women were around. He didn't change much while I was there but some time later he called for me as though something about my life was different. Again as I worked with a group in an office situation, I noticed as I walked into the room where the ladies gathered for lunch the language changed quickly as though they recognized I was different. Our lives do make a difference and you can be sure of it.

<u>Blessed are those who mourn for they shall be comforted.</u>

It is easy for us as humans to read this as referring to those who mourn the loss of a loved one. Well it could be that but it means much more. As we look at things that are happening around the world and the huge number of people that are dieing and being run from their homes we quickly begin to think of their suffering and wonder what it would be like for us. Usually we just think of the fact that it isn't happening here and are relieved that it isn't. There is that attitude again.

It is much easier to think of our own well being than to worry about someone else and their suffering. Jesus said we will be comforted because we care. Not because we send money to them or pray for them but because we care and 'mourn' for their suffering. We look all around us and no one seems to be calling for help so we go on our merry way in peace without visiting or calling to know how they are. I can remember a case where an organization was formed to minister to a certain group of people and at the end of the month a report was requested at which a member of the group said "no one came for us to help". The group was to be 'the elderly' and 'home bond'. Do we really care? Or is it just a surface thing? It is exciting to hear how our Baptist people are helping people that have faced hard times because of floods or storms. It must bring great joy to those ministers.

Blessed are the meek for they shall inherit the earth.

Some of you may remember the story of 'Casper Milktoast' If you are old enough, and remember how he was so timid that anything could happen and he would breeze right by with out any retort. Well Jesus was not talking about being 'meek' in that way exactly but in a sense He was. You know we can be timid and useless or we can be timid and wise. Jesus was timid as some people think of it but He was actually being obedient to His father. I think that is what Jesus was thinking of when He used the word meek. His thought was that if we are all obedient to the Father and follow His leading we will surely be supplied with all our needs. Not wealth but needs.

I often wonder what God thinks of those on TV and radio that brag about their ability to heal or bring good fortune. It gives me the feeling that their ego is stronger than the power of God in them. Pride may be a good thing but when you turn it into 'proud' it can become a hindrance to accomplishing God's plan. I often think some preachers say too much as they preach. I remember one preacher and pastor that usually ended his sermon in fifteen minutes or less. The message was simple and to the point and easy to understand. The church grew rapidly during his ministry. Others seem to watch the clock and keep talking till his hour is up whether he has anything to say or not. The message is lost in the 'afterthoughts'.

Blessed are those who hunger and thirst after righteousness for they shall be filled

I remember that as a child I was anxious to learn all I could. When I was in the first grade I asked for a dictionary for Christmas so I could learn words. By the time I was in third grade I had memorized that little book, or so I thought. Now at 83 I can't seem to remember any of them. I kept trying to understand new words and I found it a delight to try to know all I could. I was reading the Bible and trying to find words from the Bible and learn their meaning. Not all words in the Bible were used the same as we were using them then and that made study more interesting. I still believe the King James version is the best as someone said if it was good enough for Paul it is good enough for me and that is what I tried to memorize.

While in Malawi it became more exciting as we discovered the people there were more interested in studying the Bible than most Americans. It is bothersome to think that so many Christian people know so little about the Bible. Some know the words and even memorize much of it but don't know what it really means or how to apply it to their lives. I am convinced that we put too much importance in finishing the class time and not enough time applying the Bible to real life. While I was in the service I found very little to do during spare time so I would get out my Bible and read. I soon was joined in reading as several others found the Bible a very interesting book. At times there would be ten to fifteen service men studying with me. That was a real joy for me.

<u>Blessed are the merciful for they shall obtain mercy</u>

Mercy is often described as undeserved favor. It is difficult to understand how God can be so merciful to people that do not deserve anything as far as God is concerned. At 83 years I feel like I have received at least 13 years of undeserved mercy. I don't know why I am still on this earth but God has given me extra time for some reason. All of us have received more from life than we can ever repay. God in His mercy has given us an opportunity to enjoy life to the fullest if we listen to His teaching and apply it.

Jesus made it simple by His life on this earth and He taught His followers in several messages He delivered as He stood on the mountain side near Jerusalem. As the learned man came to Him and asked what was the greatest commandment He gave a very simple answer. "The greatest commandment is to love the Lord with all your heart, all your mind and all your soul and the next is like unto it to love your neighbor as yourself". In these two commandments lies the secret to a happy life.

Again as He taught His followers the things that really mater in life He pointed again to the idea of being servants to all. As the disciples listened to Jesus teaching He commended them for giving Him food, rest and care and they were a little surprised and asked "Lord when did we do this for you". His reply was "when ever you give a piece of bread or a drink of water to one of the least of these my children you did it unto me". Jesus came as a servant and we should be the same.

<u>Blessed are the pure in heart, for they shall see God.</u>

Pure in heart? How can anyone be pure in heart when we are all very worldly? What does 'pure in heart really mean? Can we possibly be pure? I think Jesus made it plain that all of us are sinners and only through His cleansing blood can we be clean. Because He died for us all we can trust His promise that we will be pure in God's eye. There is no other way to be pure. Thinking again of the Jewish leaders of Jesus day it is clear that the important thing to them was looking good. Standing in an obvious place to pray and be seen of man was a sure way of receiving God's blessing. Giving alms to the poor was a necessity for being considered righteous. Since the poor did not 'have' to give they were considered sinners. While at the same time the 'religious right' taking advantage of those that were in need, they tried to look righteous in the eyes of men and not knowing that God saw them in a different light.

<u>Blessed are the peacemakers for they shall be called the sons of God.</u>

As I listen to the radio and television I can not avoid wishing for a 'peacemaker' to get the world on a better track. Every day a new battle breaks out that brings misery to millions of innocent people. They are all crying for peace but it is futile. There is a passage in the Bible that says "the people will cry for peace but there will be no peace". It seems to be that way today as real peace seems to be so far away and impossible to achieve. Many organizations try to promote peace in their own way. Some with violent action and some with peaceful solutions but I fear the only peace that can be achieved in this world is when we find peace through the promises of God and Jesus Christ. Jesus said "I bring peace", "My peace I leave with you" and He wished for peace for all of His followers as He left this earth. Peacemakers are those that try to share the love of God through all their <u>actions and words</u>. As we deal with others in any way we have the opportunity to be peacemakers.

<u>Blessed are those who are persecuted for righteousness sake, for theirs is the Kingdom of Heaven.</u>

I have a thought but I am not sure I know how to express it. It is not fair to say we in America do not have persecution, for some have been persecuted for their stand for Christ. It just isn't a nationwide thing as in some countries so we don't think of people in United States of America as being religiously persecuted. We have however been limited in expression of our belief as members of certain groups that wish to consider such expression as against the constitution of the USA. I have stated my belief in this matter in other writing and wish only to relate the fact that our forefathers established this nation on Christian principles and many of them stated that when this nation veered from a faith in God it would parish.

For more on this subject you can find and read Mr. William Federers' book "Americas God and Country". I think this book should be required reading in every American school. We may be facing that fact now and especially as we enter a period of time under a new president. Maybe God wants us to face persecution so we will be reminded of His concern and His promises. The apostle Paul warned Timothy and others to stand fast in the faith because it is the only way we can find strength for facing persecution.

Perfection?

Is keeping all the Beatitudes all that is necessary to be perfect? No and neither is keeping the Ten Commandments a promise of perfection.

I don't often watch TV as I like to be busy doing things with my hands, but I have watched several preachers on Sunday and some other days and am very disappointed as I hear them beg for contributions. Some have items for sale, or as gifts for a price, and I wonder if they ever go to God for assistance. Jesus said I will supply all you needs so why do they need to beg from their listeners?

You can be a heathen, an atheist or a believer but send me the money so I can do The Lords work. I listen to one pastor often and wonder why he is so different. He never shouts as though the people are hard of hearing. He doesn't tell them they are sinners that need to be forgiven. He just shares the words of Christ and lives them daily. He knows the people that are listening are not perfect but he also knows that they are aware of their shortfalls and don't need to be reminded of them. The Holy Spirit is always there to convict and to guide and is only waiting for the repentant to acknowledge Him and follow His instructions.

The Spirit led pastor is a listener, a concerned person, one that has the hearts of the people as his greatest concern. His very life is his testimony and shows in every possible way that he cares and wants to be helpful. The words he preaches in the pulpit will be the words given to him by inspiration of the Holy Spirit and not taken from some other preacher's sermons. The pastors' life will reflect the life of Christ in every way.

What is the perfect person like? He is just like you and me but with a few traits that only He can achieve. Jesus Christ the son of God.

I wonder if any church accepts newcomers as they are or do they get scrutinized very carefully before they are received. Do they have to be the same color or the same race? I remember a story of the rather rough looking young man entering a church, and finding the seats full, went to the front of the church and sat on the floor. A rumble began in the church as people began to whisper and finally one lady told a deacon seated near by to go do something about it. Maybe escort him out. His response was to walk up and set down by him with a gesture of courtesy. A righteous deacon.

We seem to expect every one to suddenly be perfect when we all know that is impossible. As new members join the church we seem to expect them to instantly live a perfect life just like 'ours'. Who is the judge? Many pastors are treated the same way as they make a small mistake and immediately they are treated as though they are of no use to the church. The real Christian thing to do is help him grow just as we grew as young Christians. Likewise we as believers in Christ should be considerate of new Christians and help them grow. Learn to understand them and love them as they are. As Paul wrote to the Christians in Ephesus he reminded them that they were once walking in sin and had to grow to be more like Christ so we should help others to grow without condemning them. I think of an email I received a short while ago about a professor that invited others to coffee. He had set out cups of all sorts, nice fancy cups, not so fancy and even some paper cups and invited them to take a cup and enjoy it.

As he expected the first took the fancy cups and the rest took what was left. As they began to sip the coffee he reminded them of the fact that they had chosen the nice cups first. He then said you came for coffee but each looked for the best. The coffee is the same in each cup but the cup is just what keeps the coffee together. It doesn't matter what the outside may look like but the inside, or the heart, is what makes the difference.

It would be nice if we could all see others as Jesus sees them. We tend to look at the cover and not read the book.

I once advised a young lady not to buy a certain car but found she had already paid for it. The underside was badly rusted and looked dangerous but the outside was a beautiful red car. Beauty is only skin dip so I have heard. I know we have a tendency to see the outside first by nature but we need to learn to look at the heart and see what its' need is and not judge by the looks.

I think of another story that I received some time ago about a 'well-to-do church' in a large town. On a Sunday morning as the members began to gather an elderly looking man, unshaven and wearing raged clothes stood at the entrance with his head down in an attitude of fear. As the service began and they were singing a hymn that old gentleman stepped to the pulpit. The crowd was in shock as the man began to remove his old coat and hat to reveal the pastor. As the crowd grew silent he said "not one person offered to invite me in or open the door for me. Do you treat others the same"?

What does the Bible teach?
What does the Bible tell us about doing the 'will of God'? Or what is 'Gods work'?

I am sure Jesus summed it up in those two commandments as He gave them to the man who asked. "Love the Lord your God with all your heart and love your neighbor as your self." Jesus gave the story of the Good Samaritan as an example of the concern we should have for each other. Not just people like me but everyone we would touch as we go through life. It is not always easy to answer everyone's request in the way they would like but often the request is presented for our good.

I have often been asked to help someone with money or maybe with some advice. I study the person over and I try to ask God for advice knowing He has promised to help in times of need. I don't always get the answer I want but I try to be as kind and courteous as possible. I may have made some bad decisions but I think I may have helped some person in need.

One man that has been a repeated 'beggar' asked for money to take his daughter to the hospital for treatment. The story would have been good except he went on to tell me his wife had left him and he had no one to help him. His wife had been to borrow money the day before and said all was well with them. That brought an end to his request as he realized I knew he was lying to me.

While in Malawi we had the opportunity to travel to the north part of the country to visit missionaries in Mzumzu but on the way we gave a young man a ride to his home village. Leaving his village to get back to the highway became a reason for prayer. He had given us a map to get back on track but we got lost. After driving for several hours and not finding the road we came upon a hitchhiker. Georgia was very unhappy that I stopped to pick him up since many things happened that could be dangerous. However we needed help and I felt God had sent that help. This man was not only helpful he was also willing to go fifteen miles beyond his home to get us to Mzumzu safely and walk back to his home. We ministered to him but he did more for us. God is so good.

Yes I believe in angels. An experience I had while in Zambia made me a real believer as a dream came to me one night that was so real I will never forget it. My father had passed away in nineteen eighty one while we were in Malawi but now it was nineteen eighty seven. It seems we were in a gathering of missionaries for the regular monthly meeting and my father came in looking like a young man and touched me on the shoulder and just said "I have come for her". For some reason I knew my mother had also died. The next morning my brother called from North Carolina to tell me she had passed away. Without hesitation I told him I already knew it as dad had come to tell me. I am sure he was shocked but I was consoled by a God that really cares.

How do I know the will of God? Number one, you don't get it from reading this book. You don't get it from reading the Bible. The Bible is a starting point but there is more to it than that. I am sure you have heard the remark about Judas hanging himself and the words "Jesus said go thou and do likewise". No there is more to it than that. As we read the Bible it is a necessity that we let the Holy Spirit guide as we read. It is true that the Bible has all of the answers but they may be hidden to those that do not let the Holy Spirit show them how to apply it.

I think many times we let our own desires give us the answer we seek instead of listening to the Spirit. My father traveled a lot on his way to revivals and was often reminded that he should not pick up hitch hikers. Dad was not one to let an opportunity go by without checking it out. He did pick up hitch hikers many times and never had a bad experience as a result. On one occasion he picked up a young man and as they road along he asked the fellows destination and found he was hoping to go to college but was not sure he could afford it. The boy was from a rather poor family and had to make his way on his own. Dad began to tell him there was a God that could help and how he could ask Him for help.

He was invited to come to the church where Dad was holding a revival that evening and Dad would take him on to his destination after the service. He was pleased with that offer and Dad drove late that night to do as he said and felt he had accomplished what God would have him do. An effort was made to do something to help the boy and funds were donated to help him get started in college.

As years passed that young man came to visit Dad and inform him that he was now enrolled in seminary and planning to be a pastor. He was one of the first of Dads' sons in the ministry.

I often wonder how many opportunities we miss by being afraid of the next step. How many times do we miss the mark by worrying about insurance rather than listening to The Spirit? A program for youth might require that we carry more insurance and that might not be enough protection. <u>Let's just not get involved</u>. An idea may be advanced that might cost money but we shut it out because the budget has not planned for it. Have we forgotten God's promise to provide what we need?

'What would Jesus do?' has become an important question in the lives of many young people in recent years and I think we need to ask that question as each day arrives. I do think God speaks to us in many ways to direct us but one of the most overlooked opportunities is that where, walking down the street, we see something that tells us the Spirit has something there for me.

So often we want to do the 'will of God' but shut Him out by not looking or watching every moment of our life. How many opportunities have we missed?

Sometimes when we hear a preacher tell us we need to do the work of God we think he means we should be preaching. God has plans for all of us and has told us the answer to our question is right before us and all we need to do is listen for that still small voice that may be speaking through a neighbors' need. Maybe even through a 'vision' as we think of someone that may need comforting or help in some way. Maybe they just need someone to listen or to pray with them.

Paul in writing to the Corinthians reminded them that God gave each of us different abilities and talents because He needed each of us to do different things. Just like our bodies that have different parts but all work together to create life. So with the church, each of us has a different task to carry out. When every part does its' part there will be real life in the church and it will multiply.

Many years ago there was a woman in Kansas City, Kansas that never attended church but was the real backbone of the church. She was so crippled up with arthritis that she could not even get out of bed by herself but she prayed for the church, the pastor and the people. She was a very dedicated person with great concern for people.

Often we would take someone that was sad, depressed or lonely to visit her and they would quickly know that they were very fortunate and blessed.

At another church in Kansas City there was a young man that was crippled and deformed until some considered him very ugly and unattractive. Realizing people were avoiding him the pastor went to visit him and found he was in a foster home and not very well treated there so he asked him to do him a favor. This young man always had a smile and was very cheerful and the pastor asked him to stand at the door and greet people as they came in. He could not speak to hold a conversation but he could smile and say welcome. In a short time he was the real joy of the church and the church changed and began to grow. He became the miracle the church needed. It is so easy to find fault with others without considering that God has a place for them as well. God only has the privilege of judging.

Many pastors seem to think church attendance is needed to be a Christian. Some have said we should be there every time the doors open. I think those pastors are concerned about having a large crowd to listen to their great sermon. Christ said GO not come. If being in church is what God tells me to do I agree but that is not all God has for us to do. I know many people have to work on Sunday to pay the bills but if they are studying the Bible and listening for that still small voice God may have more for them to do at work than at church. Love is the most important thing for all of us. If all we do is done in love God will make use of it. If it is done for any other reason God will reject it. If I could sew God could use that. If I could paint God could use that. We all have some talent that God can make use of if we let Him.

I remember a church where the organist was an English professor at a college. She was very disturbed when the new pastor used such poor English and often tried to correct him. It was not long before she realized this pastor had a heart of gold and loved everyone including her. She went to him after the invitation was given and apologized for even thinking about his English.

God can use any and all of us if we are willing to stop and listen to that still small voice and not worry about the perfection in our life or that of others.

I worked with a man in Kansas City several years ago that always had stories to tell. One was of two fellows that worked together and had become good friends. One of them lost his job and was going to a neighboring town to look for work. They met for a last time and hugged and expressed their sorrow and one said we will always be friends to the very end. The other said yes, now can you loan me five dollars? At which the first said that <u>is the very end</u>. Do we really care?

In another case a women's missionary meeting was having a study of the needs for more missionaries. So they all prayed that the Lord would lead some of the youth of the congregation to become missionaries. Soon after, the daughter of the leader of the group came to her mother and said mother I am going to be a missionary. Instead of rejoicing the mother said "oh, no, not my daughter Lord".

How sincere are we when we commit ourselves to do the work of God?

Let's go back to the love that Jesus talked about. His love is different than what is often thought of. It is not like making a resolution as resolving to quit something or to accomplishing something. The beatitudes Jesus talked about were attitudes that are lasting, permanent and continuous. Not something we could turn off and on as needed. Jesus love was not something he decided to do because it came natural. He didn't just decide to love this person today but turn him off tomorrow. It was His nature to love. I have known people that were loving and kind to some but others they seemed to abhor or at least treat differently. That is not love but the evidence of prejudice.

We can not be 'merciful' one day and not the next or be 'merciful' to one person and not the next and think we are merciful. Love has no limitation in time or place. It is continuous or it does not exist. Many people are anxious or unsure of their salvation when the Bible tells me if we put our trust in Christ we know we are saved because Jesus never changes and we are in His hands. Jesus' love never fails.

Jesus talked to His disciples about prayer because they had seen Him praying a lot and were curious and wanted to learn more about it. As He gave them what we often call the Lord's Prayer He explained 'the procedure' or the order of prayer but it was just that. There was more to it than that. As He talked about the Pharisees, and their desire to be seen of men He made it clear that prayer was a thing that originated from the heart. Prayer is having conversation with God. It has two sides to it in that if we talk to God we also must listen to Him. Without listening it is not prayer but begging for something we do not deserve. Paul talked about praying without ceasing.

If we expect God to guide us we must listen continuously or we may miss out on the things God has for us to do. We may even miss the instructions for the moment and we need His guidance for every moment of life. Prayer is being in tune with God when we pray for a friend or neighbor. When we are attempting a difficult task or even a simple one God is ready to guide us so why leave Him out of the picture for even a moment.

You have no doubt heard preachers use the phrase "ministerily speaking" so they could make a statement that might not be totally true. There is no such occasion as God is always listening and cannot be left out. He hears and is concerned about our every thought and word. Paul, as he wrote to Timothy and others said we should not be involved in meaningless arguments or conversation but rather to speak the truth always. Let your conversation be yes or no and not meaningless. As a matter of fact our entire thought should be a part of our prayer life.

The real Lords prayer is found in John 17 where Jesus prayed for the disciples and for all that would follow Him from that day forward. His prayer was accompanied with the knowledge that He would soon be dieing on the cross for all of them and He wanted the Father to be gracious with all of them and us. His concern was real and from the bottom of His and the Fathers' heart. There was no alternative. If we are to be called Christians we will be just like Christ and willing even to die for a friend or enemy.

To expand on 'love' let us think of what love is. John 4:8 says "He that does not love knows not God for <u>God is love</u>". If God is love then love is also God. If we claim to be Godly we must also be loving and that without any variation. Proverbs 10:12 says" Hate creates strife but love covers all sins". To say we love but still hate a neighbor is a falsehood and a sin. Love has no boundaries.

The Bible is full of mysteries, from the creation story to the last of the book of Revelations. When I taught junior boys several years ago I liked to give them a reason to study the Bible and it was fun and provided a new way to learn. One of the mysteries that always stirred their interest was about the oldest man that ever lived but also died before his father. Another was who in the Bible carried the heaviest spear? Who cut his hair once a year and it weighed nine pounds?

I never gave a clue of any kind because I wanted them to look it up and that they enjoyed and learned from it.

I see several other mysteries as I look through the Bible, that are not as easy to see. Paul talked about the mystery of Christ and His love. As Jesus spoke to the multitude from the mountain side He did not have an amplifier to carry the message over the crowd.

As Peter preached at Pentecost he not only did so without an amplifier he spoke to people of several languages and they all heard and understood. Now that is a mystery. I think I experienced the same thing while in Malawi as I listened to pastors preach in Chichewa, which I did not know, but I felt the Spirit the same as those that did know the language.

What was the answer to these mysteries?
Peter was not speaking in all the different languages but they all heard and understood. Jesus

did not use a megaphone to speak to the multitude, or at least I never saw one in any of the pictures we use with children. What did take place?

   The mystery of the Holy Spirit. As Jesus spoke with His followers He said He would send a comforter who would help us with anything that we faced. I am convinced the Holy Spirit was there in each case to translate for every language. He could carry the message from Jesus to everyone gathered to hear Him speak as He stood on the mountain side, and there were probably several different languages represented there. Why do we doubt the power of the Holy Spirit? If He can carry the message in any language to anyone then He can carry His message through us if we just give Him the opportunity.

Perfection? What is Gods' perfect will for you and me? I have heard of many attempts at outreach or visitation with very few lasting more than a few weeks or months. We get discouraged when people close the door before we finish our conversation or maybe not even let us in. Where was the Holy Spirit? I fear we are going for the wrong reason or at least going at it in the wrong way. As I mentioned earlier we seem to think we should immediately be able to win someone to Christ. Forget that. <u>Jesus said GO and my spirit will go with you</u>. He did not say go with a big Bible under your arm so people could see you were a good Christian. Why must we look so pious and show those we care about that we are better than they?

There was at one time a program that involved "friendship evangelism". The main point of the study was that we are letting others see Christ through our lives continuously. Making friends is to me the only way to reach people and eventually win them to the Lord. Since there are so many false prophets amongst us it is easy to see that people of every nature are doubtful of Christians. Evangelists, some pastors and even some so-called Christians have created a very difficult situation for Christians by the wickedness they have displayed. We have to overcome these and we don't do it by being 'pious' or Mr. and Mrs. Goody. We do it with love like that of Christ. Muslim people have stated their dissatisfaction with Christians because of the adultery, fraud and other things they read and hear about. Only the life we live before others can overcome that stigma.

    I enjoy meeting new friends. Some are not so easy to get acquainted with and may take patience and time. A verse in the Bible says "wait I say on the Lord" so why do we expect to 'save anyone over night' when <u>we can not</u> <u>save anyone</u>. That is the work of the Holy Spirit and He will complete it in His time. Love and patience are the answer. Many years ago we lived half a block from a man that had a very real problem with alcohol. He would sit on his back porch after work and literally yell profanities for the benefit of the neighbors that often complained. My father went many times to set with him to chat and that would calm him down. One night the man asked Dad why he was coming up to talk to him and Dad's response was "because God knows there is a better man in you somewhere" and He wants me to find him. Love can make a big difference if God is with us. That man became a very strong member of the church in a short while.

As spring approaches we have the greatest opportunity to meet new people or neighbors. I enjoy spring as do most of us and I like to grow flowers. The flowers add a lot to life and are the perfect opening for a conversation. If I go for a walk I tend to look at the flowers the neighbors have planted or if they are out I ask what flowers they plan to plant. Is that so difficult? Why not get to know them while you are there?

As I mentioned before we are not required to win people to the Lord we just show them we care and the Holy Spirit will take it from there. He might open the door for you to give your testimony about what Christ has done for you but 'wait on the Lord and He will direct your path'.

I have seen preachers go to a home with the idea of winning the people to the Lord only to drive them farther away because the action of the preacher is not of real concern for them and they know it. We cannot hide our inner feelings. No matter how hard we try.

Stop right now and think of what God has meant to you. Maybe even write it down on the blank page 75 in the back of this book. Make it simple but leave nothing out. Relate something about when you made a profession of faith in Christ. Don't say 'the day I was saved' as some may have been saved long before they made a public profession. Some people have no idea what the term 'saved' means. When you tell someone else of your experience, the Holy Spirit will take it from there and you can feel good that you have shared it with others. Many pastors relate stories to the congregation of the experience they had as they visited with someone and that can be a great influence to the church and its' members.

Jesus had some special experience that may seem He had an advantage over us but remember He said "My Spirit will go with you" so just remember you are not alone.

I know many preachers contend that we must get a decision right away because Jesus may come at any time. I am afraid there is a stumbling block to that idea. With the news media so quick to publish any failure of a preacher or any Christian, we are faced with people who have come to doubt our religion even before we approach them. The only way we overcome that is to befriend them and show them we care just as Jesus would if it were Him here.

I am afraid our biggest problem is not being sincere. Why do we visit or try to witness to anyone if we are not really concerned about them. I remember an occasion several years ago that a man came to visit us and invite us to his church. That was encouraging to us to know someone cared.

After a short visit Georgia asked "where do you go to church"? His reply was Calvary Baptist Church where we had been attending for three months and Georgia's natural response was "we have been going there for three months and I don't remember seeing you there". I felt sorry for him and we wished afterward that her response had not been given for we never did see him in that church. He might have been sincere at his invitation but our response fully discouraged him.

Before you talk to anyone be sure you are ready for any response from the one you talk to. It is not a requirement that we know the entire bible but we need to know it well enough to talk to someone about it. In other words "study to show yourself worthy" and let God lead the way. I have seen People with a great smile but you could tell it was false. I knew one man that always had a big smile. The problem was the smile was there even when he was angry. How 'false' can we be and still minister as Jesus instructed us?

Do we really care? Do we go as though it is our duty? God knows our hearts but, maybe a surprise to you people know when we are sincere. When someone comes to your door and says "I would like to talk to you about our children", you know instantly he is selling something. What image do you leave with people? Think about it.

Most people know that the Thirteenth chapter of first Corinthians is called the love chapter. It gives us a picture of what love really is and what we must be to call ourselves the children of God and joint heirs of Jesus Christ. In 2 Corinthians 5:14 Paul uses the words" the love of Christ constrains us". We are not doing anything on our own or because it is a duty but because of the love that God and His son Jesus had for us. We are <u>compelled</u> to do just as Jesus did while on this earth. Not because the preacher told us we should or because we read it in the Bible but because of the love bestowed upon us. It is not something we have to study for but an automatic response to the Love of God.

We seem to have a great concern for members that are sick or in hospitals or maybe some that have family problems but if we don't know them we don't have to worry about them. <u>How true it is and how sad.</u>

Let us get practical. I have said some about outreach and visitation but it may be hidden to some. I think God put my church in the community where it is for a reason. He wanted a group of believers there that would demonstrate His love to the people that live there and that would latter move there.

There was a video produced by the Home Mission Board of the Southern Baptist Convention several years ago about a little rural church near Modina, Missouri, that was struggling to stay alive. A retired pastor came to help them and immediately began to go house to house to get acquainted with the farmers, business people and all he could find. His wife followed the school bus around and noted where children were let out. With that interest the members began to follow the lead and the church began to grow and became a great ministry to the community.

If the church is really doing what God put them there for they should know everyone that lives there. How else can they minister to them? When I say "know" them I mean to know their children, know their work, know of possible health problems or anything that we might be able to help them with. Remember in the book of Acts how the Christians all joined in union to stay alive. They were being ostracized and blacklisted so work was difficult to find and life was hard. They sold all they had and put it together so all would have something. They shared their belongings and the Love of God.

I know those in Paul's time were followers of Jesus and you may say that was different but I don't think so. Jesus said to love your enemies as well as your friends. No one should be exempt from our love because it is Gods' love and not just ours.

How do we get started? "In the beginning God created the earth" our beginning should be left up to God because He knows how. Yes it sounds hard to meet every one in the community but we first have to "take the first step'. You have heard that "Rome wasn't built in a day, but Nero destroyed it in a day". Well "Nero" has been busy in your community for a long time so you have a big job to overcome.

Paul reminded Timothy that he should live so no one could find fault with his life. For the same reason the church needs to be in unison so the community cannot find fault with it. How do we get started? Just like our lives, one day at a time, one house at a time but with the power and leadership of the Holy Spirit. I think as we hear of others testimony of a visit they enjoyed we find it more interesting. You never know what joy it can be till you let the Holy Spirit lead you in conversation with a new friend. *Try it, you will like it.*

That is a start at trying to reach people and build the fellowship but why do we do it? Are we trying to get them into the membership to increase the attendance? Are we trying to just do our duty? There are many good reasons to meet our neighbors and those are not good ones. We know that everyone should have the opportunity to find Christ as Savior. We want them to rejoice with us as we worship. Most of all we want them to know that we care and God cares too. He has made many promises to us in that He will help us in times of trouble and He is there to help them as well. Paul said as he wrote to the Corinthians in 2 Corinthians 4: 3 and 4, "Blessed be the God and Father of our Lord Jesus Christ, the father of mercy and God of all comfort, who comforts us in all tribulation, that we may be able to comfort those who are in any trouble, with the comfort with which we our comforted by God". It is good to make new friends whether we lead them into a church fellowship or not but it is <u>not</u> a DUTY. It is because Christ loved us and we by our Christian nature want to love them also.

The eighth chapter of 2nd Corinthians is a sharing chapter. In it Paul talks about how the early Christians shared what they had so no one was left out but all had the necessities for life. The situation then was about food and such needs but for the same reason we need to know about those all around us so we can share with them whether it be with physical needs or the needs of the Spirit. It is difficult to share the Spirit without first showing we care enough to share the possessions.

Why would God put a church fellowship in my neighborhood for people that live in another town? What purpose would it serve? God put my church in my community so I would help my friends and neighbors. He tells me I am not alone but He is with me and will guide in every attempt to help others. <u>What help are we to offer?</u> Jesus said I will go with you so put your worries aside and let my Spirit lead the way. Jesus will not fail or let us down if we are truly concerned.

I see a very real problem with many churches today because members move away to a different neighborhood but fail to move their membership. Instead they return regularly to the old home church. That would be fine normally except in most cases those members loose concern for people in that community because they are no longer a part of the community. In a matter of time the community is left without caring people to show the concern that should be there.

I remember reading an article in the paper a few years ago about an elderly woman that was approached by a young man that was running from the police. He forced his way into her home and wanted money to get away. Instead of money she told him to sit down and she would fix him food because he looked tired and hungry. He was no doubt surprised but obeyed and as he ate she told him there was a better way for him and instead of running he turned himself in to the police and thanked her for the food. God is always there to help if we just trust Him.

You may question the idea of community action and that I can understand because we have all become so self sufficient that we forget the neighbor. As I consider the present day I am very concerned about the future. In a time when the future of our nation lies in the hands of people that may have very different opinions of what our nation should be like I feel like the necessity for cooperation is very important. In another small book I wrote about the possibility that out government could very well be in the hands of those that want to destroy our democracy. The actions of a community could be the salvation of our future not only politically but spiritually as well. As Christians we have the opportunity to strengthen the spirit of our community and build a relationship that can be lasting and enduring and able to maintain our democracy as it is.

There is a sheet now available that lists talents, hobbies, abilities or any thing that a church member might use to assist a neighbor in need.

Paul talked a lot about the works of the Spirit and to me all of our abilities can be the work of the spirit if we let the Spirit show us how and when. Jesus spoke of the person that was trustworthy with the talents and he was given even more talents. I truly believe God will give us what ever abilities we need if we take the first step.

Our first step might be to have every member fill out one of those sheets so a record could be made of each member's abilities. From that could come opportunities for each of us to minister to people in need. Remember the first step is to care and be concerned and go with a smile that says I love you and God loves you.

I must take time here to state my feelings about 'target groups'. Many organizations suggest working with target groups to simplify the work but I am sure when we plan for a target group we are overlooking the ones we should be reaching. Many times the work on the target group dwindles because we have forgotten the neighbor next door that has a need as much as anyone. Jesus said we must love everyone and be ready to help and comfort all.

One large church in Texas has three 'building crews' that travel world wide to repair or build churches or needed buildings. While in Malawi a crew came from one of those churches to help build the clinic at Salima. Later some came to build the Seminary in Lilongwa. They were from large churches and had many people to go and many people to financially provide for those crews. We are not limited at our church because Jesus said if you go I will be with you so either go or you are telling God "you are not able".

Planning for an outreach program does take effort and time but can be well worth it for it will not only be carrying out God's plan it will also strengthen every individual that participates in any way. Some may not be able to do more than use the telephone and some may only be able to pray for those that 'go'. Paul wrote of the fact that God has given all of us different abilities and each has a place in ministry. In Paul's day there were seamstresses, one woman was a maker of cloth and Paul was a tentmaker. God only knows our abilities and He knows how they can be used so we just need to listen to that still small voice to find our way.

Once we have a list of names and abilities that we can put on file the next step is to let the community help decide ways we can minister to the people in the community. Yes, and I mean those that are not members. The whole point of ministering to a community is to get them involved even though they may not participate in the program. What better way is there to let them know that we care?

Begin with earnest prayer. Ask ever member to fill out the form whether they feel like they are able or not. Their concern is needed the same as one that might be more capable.

Now for some hints.

FIRST but not least you need to know the Bible. It is not a requirement to memorize it but you must know what it teaches about The Lord Jesus and what He has done for you. If you are confronted with a question about the Bible and you don't know the answer don't stumble over guessing the answer but admit you are not sure and tell them you will check with the pastor and get the answer and come again or ask the pastor to visit them. Then go home and study some more. As Paul wrote to Timothy he said don't get into needless argument.

As you all know there is a certain stigma associated with people coming to your door. When you see two young men in suits and ties, maybe riding bicycles, approach you know who they represent and are leery of them. Likewise any well dressed preacher or person carrying a big Bible can be frightful to some. There is something about strangers coming to your door that makes you want to look the other way or just not answer the door.

There is one way we can approach a home and not be a suspicious character. In my experience the most reasonable way to visit and get to know new people is for husband and wife to work together. If possible dress in casual clothes as though you are one of them and not a pious individual after something. The best visiting preacher I have ever known went visiting in his overalls and ready to help on the farm or in any way be helpful.

Remember you are going to share the love of Christ with them. They may already know Him and your visit may encourage them in their walk with Him. There may be no other reason to visit them but this is important so keep in mind that God is with you and He will direct you so go with confidence that He will do just that.

As I mentioned before the important thing to keep in mind is that people are busy and may not want to be disturbed so be considerate and ask if they have a moment so you can get acquainted. Keep the conversation brief and yet learn all you can about the family and what you or the church may be able to do to be helpful. Your life is what makes up the church so be loving and kind and God will fill in the missing points.

When it is impossible for husband and wife to go together there is still opportunity for any one to minister in Christ's name. I do not recommend that a single woman visit where she does not know the resident but there are other ways she can minister. Just ask the Lord for instructions and He will provide the way.

I remember a case where the church was not reaching out to certain people and the church was not growing. Growth of the church is not the important thing in my opinion but people need to know the Lord and every one should be on our list of concerns. I asked about a certain neighbor of the church and the pastor of the church said I don't think he is interested in our church. Are you sure he is not in need of God? I asked. No one should be left out of our ministry whether he or she is 'like us or of a different faith'. God loves them all and we should also.

I mentioned earlier the group that leaves questions in my mind about the Coming of the Kingdom. I believe the Kingdom of God comes within our hearts as soon as we accept the fact that He is the Son of God and our Savior. I also believe many people teach or make statements about

Heaven that they cannot find in the Bible. Much of this comes from hymns and not from the Bible. I take this from a previous book and hope you will think before you tell someone about the "mansion" you hope to receive.

.

Heaven?
What will it be like?

Heaven has been described in many ways. A number of TV evangelists picture heaven as a beautiful place to behold. Streets of gold, jeweled mansions, ivory everywhere. What do you think it will be like?

Paul had an experience that gave a vague picture of what he saw. He didn't say it was jeweled, golden or silver. He just said it was indescribable. Other writers have written about the beauty of heaven and some have mentioned the streets of gold but would that be necessary?

Gold is the symbol of purity. Surely the streets of heaven will be pure, but gold? Paul talked about the crown of righteousness. Yes we can expect to wear a crown. Golden slippers?

Certainly. Walking in pure steps. Heaven is not going to be what it is often pictured as, but it will be much more. As Paul said it will be indescribable.

Some talk of meeting long lost loved ones and what a joy that will be. To be back together again sounds great but is that what we can look forward to? A Pharisee came to Jesus with a tricky question that Jesus answered in His usual manner. The question was about the man whose brother had died and according to their tradition the next brother was required to take the brothers wife as his own. Other brothers died and the same tradition was required. Now he asked Jesus whose wife would be his in Heaven? Jesus answered with words that I think we should consider as an answer to our question. There will be no marriage or giving in marriage in Heaven. Who will we know and who will we look for when we get to heaven?

I am convinced that the only gold we will see in heaven will be the purity that will exist there. We will wear a crown of jewels as Paul mentioned but the jewels will be those who we influenced in life and became our brothers in heaven. We won't be looking down at those left behind since we would be looking at a sinful world and that would not be permitted in heaven. There will be no evidence of sin there. Only the glory of God and the Son sitting on the throne surrounded by the saints of all time. What greater heavenly thing could we seek?

Our sights on earth should be set on the goals Jesus set for us while He was on the earth. A drink of water (the water of Life) for the thirsty, a coat of care for the cold and homeless, a prayer of faith for those we are not able to serve personally. We should not be concerned about our rewards in heaven, they will mean very little to us when we see Jesus. What value could there be in a mansion or streets of gold? We will be too enthralled at the glory of all we see at the feet of our master.

The next question that comes to mind for me is when does heaven begin? Jesus said "bring your burdens to me and I will give you rest". Will we get to heaven or hell now? Many preachers and leaders preach about the promise of heaven and salvation from hell when Jesus said "I will give you rest". Why should we wait for the day we die and go to "heaven" to accept the promises of God? By faith we have the opportunity of a heavenly life on this earth. The right now! Not just the hereafter.

Here is a serious thought! There is a story of a lady planning to move to a new town. As she talked with a realtor about houses she became anxious about the neighborhood. So as she asked the realtor about the neighbors and the people near by, the wise realtor after a little thought replied, "what were the people like where you live now?" Her reply was just as the realtor expected, they were rude, hateful and a lot of bother. The realtor's reply was "that's the way they will be here too".

Will our life on this earth be repeated in heaven?

Think about it!

What has God done for me?

Notes; Those I have visited, those I should visit.

Contacts made

Comments

www.ingramcontent.com/pod-product-compliance
Lightning Source LLC
Chambersburg PA
CBHW021024090426
42738CB00007B/893